Clarinet

Duets for Fun

Clarinets in B♭

Easy Pieces to Play Together

Edited by Rudolf Mauz

ED 13886
ISMN 979-0-2201-3709-9
ISBN 978-1-84761-417-9

www.schott-music.com

SCHOTT

Mainz · London · Berlin · Madrid · New York · Paris · Prague · Tokyo · Toronto

Introduction

Anyone who opens this collection will be able to delight in some jewels from the repertoire for two clarinets. The book contains original pieces from the Classical and Romantic periods. Of particular appeal will surely be those duets that have been forgotten like Sleeping Beauty for almost 200 years since their original publication and have now been brought to light and made generally accessible again. One exception in this collection of original settings are three of the 'Bowling Duets' ('composed while playing skittles') by W. A. Mozart, which were originally intended for two basset horns or two natural horns.

Some of the duets I have reworked considerably, shortening over-long passages and simplifying very complicated passages. Some indications of articulation have been marked in, though not everywhere. It should be borne in mind that in Minuets the crotchets should be played fairly short. Dynamic markings have only been added in some places, while in some pieces this has deliberately been left open – as in the original.

This book is aimed at clarinettists who already have a proper basic grasp of playing their instrument. These pieces will be a valuable addition to tuition as they help to develop a sense of style and form in the interpretation of music from the Classical and Romantic periods. They will also help boost confidence in playing an individual part, aiming for evenness of tone and achieving purity of intonation. Playing duos is a valuable way of improving technique and increasing stamina. These original pieces are also very suitable for performance in concerts, auditions and competitions.

Have fun playing these duos!

Rudolf Mauz
Translation Julia Rushworth

ED 13886
British Library Cataloguing-in-Publication Data.
A catalogue record for this book is available from the British Library
ISMN 979-0-2201-3709-9
ISBN 978-1-84761-417-9

English translation: Julia Rushworth
Cover design by www.adamhaystudio.com
Cover photography: iStockphoto.com
Printed in Germany · S&Co. 9304

Contents

Duo

Amand Vanderhagen
(1753–1822)

29
f
f
p
36
f
f
p
f
42
p
mf
48
f
55
f
f
60
f
f

This page is left blank to save an unnecessary page turn.

Adagio
2
1. x mf
2. x p
5
cresc.
1.
8
2.
12
3

3 Rondo

41
f
f
49
mf
f
57
mf
67
p
mf
76
f
p
f
rit.
D.C. al Fine

Duo

Frédéric Berr
(1794–1838)

Andante

5

17
21
25
30
34

Allegretto
6
rit.
a tempo

Duo

Frédéric Blasius
(1758–1829)

Allegro moderato

7

32
40
47
54
61
68

8

Menuetto

Rondo

From the 'Bowling Duets'

KV 487/496a

W. A. Mozart
(1756–1791)

Allegro

10

From: W. A. Mozart, Bowling Duets, Schott KLB 72

11

12

Allegro

22
27
32
37
1.
2.

Duo

Frédéric Blasius

33
39
45
fp
fp
51
57
63

Menuetto scherzando

14

Trio

D.C. al Fine

Rondo

15

31
tr
37
tr
tr
f
43
49
f
55
61

Spring Morning Song

Ludwig Wiedemann
(d. 1900)

17
p
21
25
29

Woodland Shadows

Ludwig Wiedemann

17

Ludwig Wiedemann

Under the Fairytale Tree

Ludwig Wiedemann

19

17
21
mf
25
f
1.
2.
Fine
29
dolce
33
1.
2.
D.C. al Fine

A Garland of Songs

Ludwig Wiedemann

20

24
30
Moderato
37
rit.
mf
44
52

Duo

Frédéric Blasius
(1758–1829)

Allegro

21

31
37
43
49
55
61

Allegretto
22
4
Fine
9
13

18
tr
tr
22
tr
27
tr
32
37
D.C. al Fine

This page is left blank to save an unnecessary page turn.

Duo

Carl Andreas Göpfert
(1768–1818)

23

24
Allegro vivace
1.
2.

21
28
33
39
43
tr
tr

This page is left blank to save an unnecessary page turn.

Duo

Jacques Jules Bouffil
(1783–1868)

25

Rondeau

26

26
31
D.S. al 𝄌 – 𝄌
35
f
p
41
f
p
47
D.C. al Fine

This page is left blank to save an unnecessary page turn.

Duo

Carl Philipp Emanuel Bach
(1714–1788)

27

Allegro
28
dim.

31
f
p
f
37
tr
tr
42
tr
tr
f
48
p
f
53
tr
dim.
tr
59
f
tr
tr

Variations

on 'Ah vous diraj-je Maman'

Franz Anton Hoffmeister
(1754–1812)

29

Var. 2
Var. 3
Var. 4

105
110
3
115
3
121
Var. 5
129
136
145
Var. 6

153
159
165
170
3
175
183

This page is left blank to save an unnecessary page turn.

Duo

Bernhard Henrik Crusell
(1775–1838)

Andante con moto

30

31

17
20
f
23
26
30
rit.

a tempo
34
mf
40
44
f
48
51
54

About the composers

Carl Philipp Emanuel Bach (1714–1788)
Second son of Johann Sebastian Bach. Initially studied Law, then appointed as principal harpsichordist to Frederick the Great. From 1768 he was municipal director of music and cantor in Hamburg.

Frédéric Berr (1794–1838)
Studied composition with Fétis and Reicha. Clarinettist in the Parisian court orchestra and professor of clarinet at the Paris Conservatoire. Author of numerous studies and tutorial works for the clarinet.

Frédéric Blasius (1758–1829)
Clarinettist in Paris, Professor at the Paris Conservatoire. Author of a well-known clarinet tutorial work.

Jacques Jules Bouffil (1783–1868)
Studied with Jean-Xavier Lefèvre in Paris. Clarinettist in the orchestra at the *Opera Comique* in Paris.

Bernhard Henrik Crusell (1775–1838)
Born in Stockholm, studied with Franz Tausch in Berlin. Toured as a clarinet virtuoso and worked in Stockholm as a clarinettist and composer.

Carl Andreas Göpfert (1768–1818)
Studied the clarinet with Philipp Meissner in Würzburg. Studied composition with Mozart in Vienna. Clarinettist in the court orchestra in Meiningen.

Franz Anton Hoffmeister (1754–1812)
Grew up in Rottenburg; worked in Vienna as an organist und composer. Published his own compositions and works by well-known composers such as Haydn, Mozart and Beethoven.

Wolfgang Amadeus Mozart (1756–1791)
Born in Salzburg, son of Leopold Mozart, who was deputy *Kapellmeister* to the Archbishop. Early evidence of his musical gifts were carefully cultivated by his father, who took the child prodigy on numerous concert tours of Europe.

Wolfgang Amadeus Mozart was employed in the service of the Archbishop of Salzburg from 1769 to 1781, later moving to Vienna. Composer of operas, symphonies, instrumental concertos, serenades, masses, chamber music and sonatas.

Amand Vanderhagen (1753–1822)
Born in Antwerp, came to Paris in 1783. Played the clarinet in military bands and later in the orchestra of the Paris Opera. Composer and author of several tutorial works for wind instruments.

Ludwig Wiedemann (d. 1900)
German clarinettist, author of *Praktische und theoretische Studien für Clarinette* [Practical and theoretical studies for the clarinet], published in 1890.